CHOOSERS

A new play

by Holly Mallett

Published by Playdead Press 2016

© Holly Mallett 2016

Holly Mallett has asserted her rights under the Copyright, Design and Patents Act, 1988, to be identified as the authors of this work.

A CIP catalogue record for this book is available from the British Library.

ISBN 978-1-910067-43-7

Caution

All rights whatsoever in this play are strictly reserved and application for performance should be sought through the author before rehearsals begin. No performance may be given unless a license has been obtained.

This book is sold subject to the condition that it shall not by way of trade or otherwise, be lent, resold, hired out, or otherwise circulated without the publisher's prior consent in any form of binding or cover other than that in which it is published and without a similar condition including this condition being imposed on the subsequent purchaser.

Playdead Press
www.playdeadpress.com

Cuckoo Bang Present

CHOOSERS

A NEW PLAY BY HOLLY MALLETT

First performed on 17th October 2016 at the Etcetera Theatre, Camden with the following cast and crew:

Alfie: Chris Mayo
Reg: Simon Balcon

Director: Jaclyn Bradley
Produced by: Cuckoo Bang

The writer would like to dedicate this playtext to David Mallett (1938-2012).

Special thanks also to East 15 Acting School and April De Angelis – without whom, the play might have stayed as half a scene.

CUCKOO BANG

Cuckoo Bang was formed by Chris Mayo in October 2012 as a platform to showcase emerging creative talent. Their first play Between Ten and Six was performed at The Etc. Theatre (October 2012), Leicester Square Theatre (April 2013) and Brighton Fringe (May 2013). In January 2015 the company was joined by co-artistic director Holly Mallett and work began on In My Head which had development workshops at Theatre Royal Stratford East in April 2015 and its first public performances in November 2015 at The Proud Archivist in East London. Aside from productions Cuckoo Bang regularly hold workshops and networking events for emerging creatives, most recently a fight performance workshop with Dan Burman.

www.cuckoobang.co.uk | @cuckoobang

HOLLY MALLETT
Writer

A graduate of East 15 Acting School, Holly balances her time between acting and music. A professional drummer, Holly has played for a number of artists for companies including Universal Music and UK all-female collective SHE.

Acting credits include: *Elemental* (Bush theatre), NSDF award winning *League of St George* (The Hope Theatre), *London Jungle Book* (National Theatre Workshop), *CBeebies Live!* (Arena Tour) and *Shakespeare For Breakfast* (C Theatre, Edinburgh Fringe). Holly is an improviser and company manager for Waiting For The Call and is co-artistic director of Cuckoo Bang.

JACLYN BRADLEY
Director

Directing credits include: *A Midsummer Nights Dream* (Waterloo East Theatre), *Volpone* (Cockpit Theatre), *Romeo & Juliet* (Jack Studio Theatre), *Measure for Measure* (Barons Court Theatre). Other theatre work includes: *On The Edge of Me* (UK Tour) and *In My Head* (for Cuckoo Bang). Jaclyn also spent ten years as a performer and is Artistic Director of CandleFire Theatre.

CHRIS MAYO
Alfie

Founder and co-artistic director of Cuckoo Bang, Chris Mayo is an actor, comedian and writer. Theatre credits include *Romeo & Juliet* (Nuffield Theatre), *Between Ten And Six* (Leicester Square Theatre) and *Window* (Brighton Fringe), commercials include Reed, Dave, Dominos and BT and stand up work includes solo shows at Leicester Comedy Festival, Brighton Fringe and the Edinburgh Fringe.

Chris wrote and directed *In My Head* for Cuckoo Bang at The Proud Archivist and Brockley Jack in 2015 & 2016.

SIMON BALCON
Reg

Simon trained at Drama Studio London and the Actors Temple. Theatre credits include Templeton in *Charlotte's Web*, Demetrius in *A Midsummer Night's Dream*, Antonio in *Twelfth Night*, Mercutio in *Romeo & Juliet* and Reynaldo & Francisco in *Hamlet* for the Actors Temple Company. He toured nationally with Ape Theatre's *Too Much Punch for Judy*, played James in *Peckham: The Soap Opera* at the Royal Court, the Joker in *Doctor Who and the Slight Problem at Hogwarts* and Kulygin in *Three Sisters* at the Cockpit Theatre. He appeared as Gethin Price in *Comedians*, which he also co-produced.

Author's notes

The play was written to be performed by two actors in a naturalistic manner but is open to other adaptations and site specific productions.

The backstory for the character Reg has been left deliberately vague and I invite the actor to fill in the blanks as they wish.

The following text was correct at the time of print but may vary from future productions.

Characters:
Alfie – 19
Reg – Unspecified age. Older.

Choosers

A park. Evening. The audience take their seats to a stage with a man asleep under a tatty old rug. He uses a small cloth bag as a pillow. He slumbers.

A younger, better presented man appears carrying with him a pillow, a sleeping bag and a plastic bag of food. He carries a backpack on his back. He looks around nervously, sees the slumbering man, turns to leave, hesitates, decides to stay and quietly drops his belongings a safe distance away from the other man on the other side of the stage. He quietly unpacks his sleeping bag, gets in, produces a copy of "Great Expectations" and begins to read.

Lights out.

Scene 1.

The park, afternoon. Reg sits in his 'spot' looking out into the distance with a blank look on his face. Alfie sits some distance away looking awkward. He keeps sneaking glances at Reg, trying to find an opening and catch his eye. Reg stoically avoids his gaze.

Alfie goes to speak. Stops himself.

Beat.

Tries again but thinks better of it. Clears his throat quietly. Reg looks at Alfie who quickly looks away sheepishly, playing with his shoe laces.

Silence.

Alfie: Um...

[Pause. No response.]

Um excuse me... *[clears throat]*

[Reg turns to him slowly. Blankly.]

Um, hi.

[No response. Reg turns away again]

I erm, hope you don't mind but well I... I couldn't help noticing that, well um - you seem to be ignoring me...

[Again, no reply]

Not meaning to be rude or anything, but um, well, you see, you always seem to be here, there, in that spot and, even when I go to get food, or go for a walk or... well, anyway this is clearly your 'patch' isn't it, and you've probably been here a while... or not, you know. But, and I mean, far be it from me to try and take anything away from anyone, but it seems I've settled here too and well, I don't really have anywhere else to go. I guess you're probably wondering where I'm going with this, and well, it's not that I'm trying to impose or anything – a man needs his space I mean why else would a man decide to live like this? Not that there aren't plenty of valid reasons for a man to live like this other than space which now I think about it seems rather trivial, or that this isn't a wonderful place... or even that a man has to choose... but anyway you, here, there in your spot, living your life, It's great, really it's great – and any reason to be here is fine. Good even. Great! Whatever you chose must be right for you. And who's...

Reg: What do you want?

[Alfie is taken aback by Reg's sudden vocalisation]

Alfie: Oh, well, yes. What I was trying to say...look I know you got here first, I know this is your space and, your spot, over there, and I don't want to intrude, never want to intrude. But I guess, well I'm here now and maybe that's what it is, or what it might be perceived to be. Intruding. And I don't want you to think it's that. But maybe it is and that's not what I want, for you, you and for me and um... I mean no-one likes intruders do they? And I don't want you to think that's what I am because... because I want... you see I never... I *really* don't want you to think... I don't want that at all and, well, I've been here for three days now and you haven't said a word, and really I just wanted to make sure you didn't think that... I mean, I just wanted to check you're ok and happy with me being here and that you're not gonna like, you know... kill me in my sleep or something...

[Alfie trails off, not knowing what else to say]

I've offended you. Sorry. I'll pack -

Reg: I'm not gonna kill you in your sleep.

Alfie: *[relieved]* Well that's good to know. Thank you for...preserving my life. I appreciate it.

[Alfie smiles at Reg who is no longer looking at him]

So I guess this is home.

[Reg shifts his position slightly but says nothing]

Do you stay here all year?

[again no reply]

How long have you been here? This is my first time, you know, sleeping out on the streets. Well, this is a park isn't it, so I guess it's more sleeping out on the path. Or under a tree. This is the first place I came after, you know after... leaving home and all that. I left in the morning and well... found myself here. Strange.

[silence]

Gosh it's cold. Is it always this cold? Even in the summer? You forget how cold nights can be when you're in a house or halls. All the same the temperature seems a bit harsh for March. *[rubs his hands together]* Is it always this bitter?

Reg: Yeah.

Alfie: Oh.

Reg: You get used to it.

Alfie: You do?

Reg: Yeah.

Alfie: That's good.

> *[A silence falls again. Alfie takes his backpack, unzips it and starts to remove the contents, glancing at each object as he removes it, checking he has everything he brought with him.]*

Reg: What you got?

Alfie: Oh just some stuff I packed before I left. Nothing valuable. Random bits, don't know why I packed most of it to be honest... Guess I figured I'd better take at least something with me to remind me of home.

Reg: Where's home?

Alfie: Farnham.

Reg: That's far.

Alfie: Well, Portsmouth really I suppose. That's where I left from anyway. I go to Uni there. Or I did...

> *[beat]*

Reg: Why'd you leave?

Alfie: It's complicated. Not sure I could even say... complicated...

Reg: Always is.

Alfie: Yeah. Were you from around here? You know, before you left.

Reg: Nah.

Alfie: Oh, ok.

[beat]

Look um, I never really got to introduce myself. I'm Alfie. Alfred James Dean. I'm 19. Fresh out of...

Reg: James Dean..?

Alfie: Yeah I know right? Ridiculous isn't it...

Reg: Yeah a bit.

Alfie: James was my Great-Grandfather, he was in the Navy, died when he was 22, fighting. Honour's a pretty big thing in my family. I was named after him. Hey, I still don't know your name.

Reg: Reg.

Alfie: That short for anything?

[No reply]

Reg it is. Well hello Reg.

[No response. Alfie gets up and starts rummaging in some bushes beside him]

It's rather strange all this isn't it really, I mean cool, but strange. I feel kind of free. Like I could just get up tomorrow and move on and go anywhere I like but

I choose to stay here, dunno why, but I do. I've got nowhere to be because I chose to leave and now it's just me out in the open on my own... and you of course, now you're here too. Or I guess I'm here too because really I only just got here and you've been here for a while...

Reg: What are you doing?

Alfie: Hm?

Reg: What are you doing?

Alfie: *[turns round and says in an over-the-top voice]* "I'm waiting for Godot!"

Reg: What?

Alfie: Hm?

Reg: I don't know what that is...

Alfie: No, of course not sorry.

[beat]

Reg: You're not one of those religious types are you?

Alfie: Huh?

Reg: Because if you are I'm not interested ok? And I don't own a Bible so there's no point quoting it at me because I'm not interested.

Alfie: Wait... what?

Reg: I'm sick to shit of bible-bashers walking the streets looking for homeless people to take under their wing. You impersonating us now? Well fuck you. I made a habit of not going in churches for 7 years and I ain't breaking that now. So you can keep your leaflets and you can shove 'em up yer self-righteous arsehole. Fuck off.

[Silence. Alfie stands stunned and confused]

Alfie: Ok wow...

Reg: What?

Alfie: Where did that come from?

Reg: Just fuck off and leave me alone.

Alfie: What..? Dude I was getting some food. *[goes back to the bush, fishes out a plastic bag half-filled with food and shows it to Reg]* I'm hungry.

Reg: What?

Alfie: I'm hungry, not religious.

Reg: Well what was that shit about God?

Alfie: What God?

Reg: You said.

Alfie: I did? Oh! You mean Godot?

Reg: Whatever, you ain't gonna find him here.

Alfie: No, no it's a play!

Reg: What?

Alfie: "Waiting for Godot," It's a play, by Samuel Beckett. It's about two tramps waiting for this guy only he never comes. But they keep waiting and no-one knows why, and it's a line from the play.

Reg: Oh.

Alfie: Silly really I mean why would you care about Beckett?

Reg: You calling me dumb?

Alfie: No, no of course not! It's just not really something that everyone would know. Absurdist plays. Books and shit.

Reg: I like books.

Alfie: Ok, well, good.

Reg: Mysteries and stuff. Stephen King.

Alfie: Ah wicked! I loved his stuff growing up. You ever read "It?"

Reg: Yeah.

Alfie: It's my favourite. Read it first when I was twelve, scared me shitless, couldn't get past chapter one. I don't give a fuck if it floats down there mate I ain't goin' in!

Reg: Carrie.

Alfie: Never read that one. My parents went to see the musical though. Jokes. Imagine that pig's blood scene as a chorus number, no-one wants to see that. Liked the film though, Oh and 'Shawshank' too, 'Shawshank Redemption.' It was based on a Stephen King. Classic film! You should definitely watch that.

Reg: Might be a little hard.

Alfie: How come?

[Reg looks at Alfie, then out to his surroundings]

Oh. Yeah, forgot about that. No TV here. Guess I'm still getting used to the change. No internet, no heating, no phone. Not once I've run out of battery anyway.

Reg: No.

Alfie: I think I've still got about 2 hours before I'm completely cut off from the world. But I'd like to keep it around for a while, y'know. Just in case.

Reg: 'Case of what?

Alfie: Oh nothing.

Reg: Second thoughts?

Alfie: No. Well maybe, I dunno. Just, in case. Always best to be safe, y'know, just in case.

[beat]

In fact maybe I should send a text home, let them know I'm ok. I mean I left a note and everything and told them that I'd gone but, you know, they'll be worrying and...

Reg: No.

Alfie: What?

Reg: Don't.

Alfie: Why?

Reg: They might track your sim.

Alfie: Someone's been watching too much TV! *[catches himself]* They can really track your sim?

> *[beat]*

Shit, I literally have no idea how the real world works. I guess not then. *[he switches off his phone]* Wow. I really am... this is it isn't it. I mean this is it. Strange...

> *[a silence falls as Alfie ponders the true gravity of what he has done.]*

Reg: Five years.

Alfie: *[snaps out of his thoughts]* What?

Reg: You asked how long I've been here. Five years.

Alfie: Oh.

Scene 2.

The park. Evening. Alfie and Reg are hanging around. Alfie sits leaning against a lamp-post reading a battered copy of a local newspaper.

Reg sits with his rug over his legs and is immersed in cleaning his nails.

Alfie chuckles to himself, distracting Reg from his task.

Reg: What? *[beat]* What?

Alfie: Hmm? Oh, nothing, I was just reading my horoscope. According to this things are gonna start looking up for Alfie Dean. Check it out. *[reads]* 'You may have been feeling somewhat stuck in a rut recently,' – fair point, pretty accurate thus far – ' Fear not, for the entrance of an important figure in your life will soon have you back on your feet and on the right track.' Well hussah, not too shabby. Maybe it's you.

[Reg continues to pick at his fingernails]

When's your birthday? I'll read yours.

Reg: July.

Alfie: July the...

Reg: 28th.

Alfie: Really? What year?

Reg: Why does that matter?

Alfie: It doesn't, I mean, well my brother was born on the 27th. '86 I think, maybe. He's older than me... yeah '84? No '86. I dunno, I thought...

Reg: Are you gonna read the stupid thing or not?

Alfie: Yeah sure um, one moment. So you're a Leo then. Leo... ah here, um, 'Times are changing and you will soon be put in a position where you risk losing something – or someone – of great value to you. Tread carefully, or you may lose more than you bargained for.'

[beat]

Ouch.

Reg: Let me see that. *[snatches paper from Alfie and scans page]* This is last Wednesdays paper.

Alfie: Oh is it? *[takes paper back]* So it is. Ah well no harm, doesn't mean it isn't still valid.

Reg: What?

Alfie: Well, just because it's an old paper, doesn't mean the horoscope can't still be right.

Reg: Yes it does.

Alfie: What? Why? It's talking about the future, how do you know that future hasn't happened yet?

Reg: Because that's not how horoscopes work.

Alfie: How do you know? What, are you some, horoscope expert? Got a degree in Mythical Astrology hidden under that rug?

Reg: I know because I know, ok? You can't go by a horoscope that's a week old.

Alfie: Why not?

Reg: Because they don't work like that!

Alfie: But how do you know that? How do you know it's not by the day you read it, and because I read it today, it activates it from now?

Reg: That's not how it works.

Alfie: But how do you *know?*

Reg: It's just not alright?

[pause]

Alfie: I think it is.

Reg: Are you fucking serious? Are you seriously trying to have this argument?

Alfie: It's not an argument, it's a debate...

Reg: Are you alright in the fucking head?

Alfie: Yes...

Reg: A horoscope, kid, is based on a star-sign which is based on the stars, in the sky, at one specific point in time! That's why it's a fucking horoscope!

Alfie: So?

Reg: The minute you take it out of that time it ain't even a horoscope anymore it's a fairytale! They all are. And they dress it up in fancy language and make it vague enough for anyone to relate and then they sell it to the papers who sell it to the public for people like you to lap up like dogs! And you do, you fucking do, every day like fucking idiots and you believe that these things make any fucking sense and they don't! It's all a fucking joke.

Alfie: Jesus Christ, sweary, why do you care so much?

Reg: I don't.

Alfie: Is this about the religion thing again, because I already explained that and anyway I'm pretty sure horoscopes would be considered blasphemous...

Reg: Just leave it alright.

Alfie: Ok, Ok. *[pause – In a surly voice]* 'Mars is bright tonight.'

[Reg looks at Alfie]

I may or may not have just quoted Harry Potter. You... won't know Harry Potter. You might actually know Harry Potter.

[Reg shakes his head in disbelief]

Seriously though it is a nice night, look. Clear. I never really noticed the sky before, not properly, not since

I grew up. I guess you notice it more out here. I guess you have the time.

Reg: It's murky as fuck. No stars, we might as well be in New York – Without the culture... or the weather.

Alfie: I heard their weather's actually quite a bit like ours. Colder even, in the winter. You ever been?

Reg: 'Course I haven't.

Alfie: 'Course. So why do you hate horoscopes so much?

Reg: I don't. I just don't see the point. I don't have time for destiny, it doesn't make any sense. There is no fate, there is no God, it's just life, and then it's death.

Alfie: That's a fairly morbid outlook.

Reg: And why would I have any other?

Alfie: I dunno. Because it's nice?

Reg: And will it be nice in five more years when I've been here ten and nothing's changed?

Alfie: You don't know that nothing will change.

Reg: Yes I do.

Alfie: How?

Reg: Because I know how the world works.

Alfie: And?

Reg: It's predictable.

Alfie: And?

Reg: And it's not a nice place.

Alfie: I guess it's not... and, maybe this whole horoscope thing is dumb – it is dumb – but it passes the time.

Reg: That it does. So you have a brother?

Alfie: Yeah, Mark. He's in the Marines. Went to Uni and everything; same one as me. Only he made it more than a year. I only went to that damn Uni to be nearer him. I guess it didn't matter in the end.

Reg: Do you miss him?

Alfie: Yeah.

Reg: You'll be alright.

Alfie: Will I?

Reg: Yeah.

Alfie: Thanks.

> *[silence. Neither Alfie nor Reg have anything else to say. Alfie takes his backpack, opens it and produces a wallet. He opens it. It's empty apart from a pound coin, a ten pence piece and a few coppers. Hidden inside is a folded piece of paper. He takes it, disregards the wallet and the coins, unfolds the paper and looks at it.]*

Reg: That your family?

Alfie: Yeah. *[hands Reg the piece of paper]* Mum, Dad and Mark outside my house. Well, my old house. That's Gran on the left there too, only she doesn't live with us anymore. And if you look carefully you can see my cat, Ringo, that's his tail in the bottom right corner. He ran off just before the shot was taken, that's why Dad looks so pissed off. We got another shot with him in it but this one makes me laugh.

Reg: Where's you?

Alfie: I took it.

Reg: Quaint.

Alfie: Ha yeah. It's a bit gay I know -

Reg: It's not gay.

Alfie: No.

Reg: You keep it in your wallet all the time?

Alfie: Nah. I used to have a picture of my girlfriend Jenny but we broke up so I took it out before I came to Uni. Then when I left I grabbed a few things and I guess this was one of them. I don't know why, silly really carrying round a photograph. And I don't know why this one. Silly. Like you said, I'm not even in it...

Reg: You can tell a lot about a man by what he brings with him.

Alfie: Yeah?

Reg: What else you bring?

Alfie: You mean other than chocolate bars and a pen knife? Let me see... *[rummages and takes out objects as he lists them]* we've got deodorant, toothpaste... tooth-brush of course. *[produces tooth-brush with a flourish]* A couple of tee shirts, spare pair of jeans, cap. Pretty boring really... oh, shit, why is this in here?

Reg: What?

Alfie: It's the pass I needed to visit Mark in his garrison a few weeks ago. You need to carry them around to prove you're allowed on the base, I must have brought this bag.

Reg: Why do you need a pass?

Alfie: Well it's the Marines isn't it. It's a matter of self-defence, you need to know who's on your grounds at all times. You know I went to Portsmouth for two reasons really. One was because my Dad wanted me to; the other was because of Mark.

Reg: Why'd your Dad want you to?

Alfie: Because that's where Mark went. If my Dad had had his way I'd have studied Engineering like Mark did, but I wanted to study English and Psychology. He used to call 'em namby-pamby subjects for lawyers and queers. Still, I didn't exactly prove him wrong did I, it was hardly a success. Anyway, so I go to Portsmouth to be nearer to Mark but I only got to see him twice in the end, in six months, and once was at home in Farnham over Christmas! The other, it says here, was 22nd Jan, almost a month and a half ago. I went to his garrison, we had a pint in the bar and he had to go two hours later. Summoned for duty or something. We never left the site, and I haven't seen him since...

Reg: You look up to your brother.

Alfie: Was that a question or a statement..? Yeah, I do.

Reg: You say goodbye?

Alfie: Left a note if that counts. Told 'em Uni isn't for me, Portsmouth isn't for me, need a bit of time... something shit like that. Told them I loved them and this was my decision, and I was ok. I highly doubt they bought any of it for a second... Did you leave a note?

Reg: No.

Alfie: So you said bye in person?

Reg: No.

Alfie: So, what? You just left?

Reg: Doesn't matter.

Alfie: I think it does.

Reg: Doesn't.

Alfie: Why not?

Reg: Long time ago.

Alfie: So..?

Reg: *[sternly]* So it doesn't matter anymore... What else you got?

Alfie: Well I think I've shared quite a lot. What have you got?

Reg: What?

Alfie: Well you must have a bag. What's in that? What great things can I 'learn about a man' by what you brought?

Reg: Nothing.

Alfie: What? Nothing?

Reg: Nothing.

Alfie: Absolutely nothing?

Reg: Nope.

Alfie: Surely you have something...

> *[Reg pulls out a small cloth bag from under his rug and hands it to Alfie who examines its contents. He pulls out a packet of crisps, a plastic knife and an opened packet of mint chewing gum.]*

This is it? This is everything you have?

Reg: Yep.

Alfie: Fuck. That... that's...

Reg: Yeah.

Alfie: Fuck.

   [beat]

Reg: Carry on.

Alfie: What? Oh, my bag. Let me see... *[rummages and pulls out "Great Expectations"]* Dickens. "Great Expectations." I think that if I had to read one book for the rest of my life this would be it... and hey, it's quite possible that might be the case. Ha. Anyway...

   [continues to rummage around]

Well I've got my keys... for the house and keys for my uni room. Pretty useless now, and um, well, that's it really. That's all. *[shocked]* Shit. I brought almost nothing... I barely brought anything with me. It's all still in my room or at home.

   [pause]

Fuck.

Scene 3 –

Reg is sitting alone onstage looking out over the audiences' heads into the park. Alfie appears from stage right carrying his pillow under one arm, his copy of 'Great Expectations' and a plastic bag in the other. Reg does not look away.

Alfie: What are you doing?

Reg: People watching.

Alfie: Fair enough.

Reg: Where you been?

Alfie: Oh just sitting on that bench round the corner having a little read.

Reg: Why?

Alfie: Well, sometimes it's nice to get a bit of a walk, change of scenery you know. It's pretty over there by the pond. In fact, why didn't you choose to stay over that side of the park anyway? Why here?

 [Reg shrugs]

 I mean why not stay somewhere nicer? Somewhere nearer the gate?

Reg: They move you if you're by the gate. They clear you away, but they let you stay if you keep a bit further in – leave you alone.

Alfie: Oh, ok. That makes sense...

Reg: What's in the bag?

Alfie: Goodies of the highest order!

> *[pulls out a bag of crisps, a pack of sausage rolls and a large bar of chocolate]*

Our banquet awaits.

> *[opens the pack of sausage rolls and throws one to Reg.]*

Reg: How'd you afford this?

Alfie: Good question. Funny story actually. Well I went for a walk in the sunshine to stretch my legs and because it's such a lovely day… and that bench round the corner – it's a really nice place to sit in the shade and just chill. So I was sitting there reading my book and I noticed that someone had dropped a bunch of change. Only about 20p in fives and coppers but still, one man's trash… so I popped it in my cap to see what would happen and carried on reading. Well, you know what I get like while I read and –

Reg: /No I don't

Alfie: - put it this way, there's no point talking to me, I might as well not be there. So I was reading my book engrossed in the wonderful world of Mr. Dickens and – I had a lovely time – and, well when I next looked up the hat was half full. By the time I'd finished three chapters I'd made about three pounds. That's a pound a chapter! Turns out begging is a lucrative business. Who knew...

Reg: You shouldn't beg.

Alfie: But that's the thing, I didn't even technically beg!

Reg: Still shouldn't.

Alfie: I didn't even realise people were dropping money in my cap! What was I supposed to do anyway? Go around the whole park asking every man woman and child if this is their money and giving it all back saying "I'm terribly appreciative and all and I could really use the money but, I wasn't actually begging so you can have it back. I'm not actually homeless, you see..." – Well um, actually I am.

Reg: Ok point proven.

Alfie: *[surprised that he actually won a round]* Wow. Really? Cool. So...

Reg: Just take it easy alright?

Alfie: Sure. Anyway, why shouldn't I beg? It's not like I have any other firm source of income...

Reg: Just doesn't feel right.

Alfie: So you're telling me in however many years you've been living on the streets – five in this park – you've never begged?

Reg: No.

Alfie: No?

Reg: No, I have.

Alfie: And..?

Reg: Just didn't feel right...

Alfie: Ok...

Reg: But it's your life. You do what you gotta do.

Alfie: I guess I do... oh, I forgot about the best bit of my walk of joy! You know that tree where all those kids hang out doing all sorts of unspeakable things? Well look what I found...

[brings out a scruffy can of beer with a flourish]

Tadaa! I hold in my hand a beautiful, unopened, less-than-premium can of hoppy goodness! Yes it doesn't have a ring pull, it may be a little warm and will most likely fizz up in my face but hey, beggars can't be choosers – ha... jokes. Hey come on I'll get my penknife, it's the only way I can see us getting into this without the ring – we'll share it. Dad always said that knife would come in useful someday, not sure this is what he meant...

Reg: I don't drink.

Alfie: What? Really?

Reg: Really.

Alfie: Oh my God why!?

[no answer]

Jesus I've never wanted a drink so much in my life! Don't you ever fancy a beer?

[Reg shrugs]

Seriously man, are you telling me that in the cold winters, when it's snowing and freezing and you're still here, you wouldn't kill for a shot of vodka to warm you up? Did you ever drink?

Reg: Gave up.

Alfie: Why?

Reg: Doesn't matter.

Alfie: Oh well, more for me.

[goes to bush where he keeps his belongings, takes out penknife from bag and begins to try to open the can]

You don't have a problem with me drinking it do you? You're not like... a recovering alcoholic are you?

Reg: Not exactly.

Alfie: What does that mean?

Reg: It means drink away.

Alfie: Oh. Ok. *[continues to work on can]* I am crap with these things. Thank God I never joined the Marines.

Reg: Give it here.

Alfie: Nah it's cool. I need to learn anyway, if I'm gonna be Mr. At-one-with-nature and all that. I'll get there. I just hope there's still some beer left in the can when I do... oh hussah here it is!

[he manages to pierce a hole in the top of the can]

Like a pro. And barely spilt a drip! Come to me sweet low-percentage goodness. *[takes a gulp, grimaces, spits it out]* Eurgh, that beer is waaarm! Knew I should have let it cool down. Well that's disappointing. *[puts the can down beside him]* So, you were people watching.

Reg: Yeah.

Alfie: I used to love doing that in pubs. I guess it's kind of the same, only with walls, and windows, and... beer that isn't the temperature of my own blood. And the reason for this people watching hobby of yours is of course...

Reg: It passes –

Alfie: Passes the time. Right. And my guess is you've been at it since I went for my walk?

Reg: No.

Alfie: Fair enough, well why stop playing now? People watching is always more fun in a pair.

Reg: Really?

Alfie: Well it is when I'm here anyway. So, who've you seen before? Got any locals? Her *[points out into the auditorium]*, I bet she comes here often. I bet that dog's pissed up every tree in this park. Then again, so have you...

Reg: No.

Alfie: Ah so first-timer, interesting. I'm thinking bored of walking the same roads every day or... *[Reg opens his mouth to respond, Alfie ignores him]* no, wait, she just smiled at that businessman eating lunch on the bench. Let's see, she's got nice shoes on, and lipstick, no sign of a poo bag... that's it! Here we have a perfect case of lonely woman syndrome. She spots a handsome stranger who lives on her street. Nice house nice car well-tailored suit – notices the park he always goes to for his lunch and voila, time for walkies. Oh I'm good.

Reg: No you're not.

Alfie: Unnecessary.

Reg: And no I haven't pissed on every tree in the park. I go to the pisser down the road same as you. And that lady, she comes here a lot. So does he. They smile, sometimes they say hi, she moves on. That's it. And they dress well because this is a nice neighbourhood. The estate's the other side of the park.

Alfie: Wow, you are absolutely no fun at this.

Reg: I don't make up stories, I just watch.

Alfie: For what?

Reg: People. The way they are.

Alfie: Boring!

Reg: So? When you put them together they make a good picture.

Alfie: I guess they do..?

Reg: The way they ignore each other. Or not. You don't have to make up their stories, it's written all over their faces.

Alfie: Wow, that's deep. Clearly you and I play different games.

Reg: It's not a game. It's just watching. You learn to read people.

Alfie: You do?

Reg: People don't tend to pretend when they're not being watched. And those that do are either bad at it, or not to be trusted.

Alfie: But they are being watched.

Reg: They don't know that. People don't tend to think of you as another person when you live on the streets.

Alfie: Is that so... you must see a lot.

Reg: Enough.

Alfie: You must learn a lot about people.

Reg: Enough.

Alfie: Ok, so tell me about her. *[points in a different direction to last time]* what can you see there?

Reg: She comes here a lot too. She's just finished her shift at Starbucks.

Alfie: You got all that from a woman in a blue vest top?

Reg: I've seen her working, she does the opening shift on Wednesdays and she gets off about this time.

Alfie: Oh, sorry. Go on.

Reg: She's having a bad day.

Alfie: How do you know that? You can barely see her face.

Reg: Posture.

Alfie: Wow, you are good! Tell me then, what about me?

Reg: What about you?

Alfie: When you first saw me, when I first came.

Reg: You came while I was asleep.

Alfie: But the next morning. The next three days.

Reg: Dunno.

Alfie: Oh come on, tell me please. I won't be offended.

Reg: Scared. Lonely. Young. Obvious first timer. Probably having second thoughts about running away.

Probably wondering whether it was the right thing to do.

Alfie: Probably. But isn't that something that's true of a lot of people like us?

Reg: You'd be surprised how many people choose this. Not everyone's a charity case. Not everyone wants to be found.

Alfie: And me..?

Reg: You what?

Alfie: Did I want to be found?

Reg: You tell me.

Alfie: Probably. Maybe. To be honest I didn't know what I was feeling that day. Or the day after that or the day after that...

Reg: It takes a while for a lot of people to understand why they go.

Alfie: And you?

Reg: I went because I chose to.

Alfie: And?

Reg: And I never looked back.

Alfie: Oh.

Reg: I'm not everyone though.

Alfie: No.

> *[silence]*

Reg: You wanted to go home.

Alfie: What?

Reg: The first three days. You kept looking at your bag; you looked at your keys. You were restless. Every night you looked at the sky and you closed your eyes. It's what people do when they're imagining they're somewhere else.

Alfie: Wow, you *are* good.

Reg: I've spent a long time being an observer.

Alfie: I can imagine you have.

Reg: I can see when people start to change.

Alfie: Yeah?

Reg: It's palpable.

Alfie: Yeah.

> *[beat]*

Reg: Do you still want to go home?

Alfie: *[ponders – comes to an unexpected realisation]* You know what? I don't think I do...

Scene 4 –

The park. Afternoon. Reg sits reading a scrunched-up paper. Alfie rushes on, distraught.

Reg: What's wrong with you?

Alfie: They stole my fucking pillow.

Reg: What?

Alfie: They stole. My fucking. *Pillow!*

Reg: They stole your pillow...

Alfie: THEY STOLE MY FUCKING PILLOW!

Reg: Who stole your pillow?

Alfie: *They* did! Those kids who hang out round the corner. The ones who drink and smoke weed round the back of that tree. They came up to me with their stupid hoodies and stupid caps and stupid baggy trousers and *stupid* gold chains with the money sign on and the rings and the cassette-tape belts and, and one of them sat down next to me while I was reading my book and asked for a light and I said – very polite like – 'sorry. I don't smoke,' and he laughed – I didn't know why – and said 'well in that case' all smirky-like and I was all in that case what? I mean, it didn't even make any sense! And I was about to politely inquire as to what the 'case' might be and what, in any case, the said 'case' had to do with me, when he pushes me off the bench, grabs my pillow, hits me with it and runs away! He takes my pillow, hits me with it and fucks off laughing with his friends. The very flippin' pointlessness of it all! I mean what's he gonna do with it? Fill it up with baccy and smoke the damn thing? Roll up a thread-count doobie? It's a fucking *pillow!* I needed that pillow. *He* didn't! Why did he need my pillow? I bet he has loads of pillows! On a big plushy bed all covered with squashy throws and cushions and little cuddly gangsta bears! I mean how would he like it if I broke into his house, went into his room and took his bed? Bet he'd stop laughing then. Bet he'd be really bloody upset!

[slumps down]

Cunt.

[pause – Reg starts to chuckle]

What?

Reg: If you could hear yourself kid...

Alfie: What do you mean?

Reg: Nothing.

Alfie: And I'm not a kid...

Reg: Oh really?

Alfie: Yes really.

Reg: You're not a kid?

Alfie: No. I'm 19 and I'm a man.

Reg: And a man would have let some weedhead little brat steal from him in a park?

Alfie: I didn't *let* him...

Reg: You've got a lot to learn.

Alfie: About what?

Reg: About life. And the people in it.

Alfie: Yeah well, I think I've had enough exposure to people like *that* for a fair few...

Reg: People like what?

Alfie: You know. People like *that*. Little dickheads who sit around all day smoking weed and polluting the atmosphere and like stealing from people just for the fun of stealing. Who flounce around in their high-top shoes going 'oh look at me I'm so fucking gangster and hard I can steal a man's pillow,' and laugh about it with their friends who are – incidentally – wearing *exactly* the same outfit in a different colour and agree that yes, stealing a pillow from a man less fortunate than them is a good way to spend an afternoon... What were they doing there anyway? It can't even be two o-clock, but they're always there, smoking and drinking and doing other no-doubt criminal things – what do they do all day? God-forbid go to school! They've gotta be what, 15? I bet they've never even *seen* a text-book, let alone understand basic arithmetic! GO GET SOME GCSE'S! Instead of stealing pillows from a homeless man! Stupid – Uneducated – Twats!

Reg: Shouldn't you be in school right now? Exercising your 'superior mind?'

Alfie: That's different. That's Uni.

Reg: Is it?

Alfie: I'm talking about basic English and maths! And anyway, that's not the point...

Reg: Why not?

Alfie: Because it's not. I'm not debating the merits of further education – those guys probably don't even think what they did was wrong! They think it's funny to take another man's bed! They are the fucking scum of the earth and everything that's wrong with our society!

Reg: Isn't that us?

Alfie: What?

Reg: Scum of the earth.

Alfie: I've never stolen a thing in my life!

Reg: So?

Alfie: So I'm nothing like them!

Reg: So they have a house, a home, and parents who pay their taxes -

Alfie: Well I wouldn't be surpr –

Reg: At least they have a bed they can put their pillow on. What about us? What do *we* give society? You can't judge people anymore Alf. You can't call people the fucking scum of the earth, 'cause now you're one of them.

Alfie: But I...

Reg: It doesn't fucking *matter* Alfie! No-one fucking *cares!* It doesn't matter that we don't steal, or even beg. It doesn't matter that we wouldn't do anything to harm anyone else or that we'd give our left fucking leg to help one of our own. It doesn't matter who the fuck we are because we are not people to them. We're wall-hangings at best. We're extras in everyone else's lives. A statement of intent for every do-gooder in the sodding world and a reminder to everyone else their life ain't that bad 'cause at least they're not us. Schaden-fucking-freude. It's the bloody mantra of the earth and the destiny and lot of every last one of us. At best? Another fucking tramp, another hungry stomach only worth feeding to save your own soul. At worst? Well you tell me...

Alfie: The scum of the earth...

Reg: The mutha-fucking scum of the earth.

   [beat]

Look, I've seen better people than those kids do despicable things to a man in need. You only have to read the news to see all the shit that goes on in this world. Just be thankful you only lost a pillow.

[silence]

Alfie: Is that really how they see us?

Reg: Yeah.

Alfie: Has anything like this ever happened to you?

Reg: Yeah.

Alfie: Does it get easier?

Reg: Yeah.

Scene 5.

Alfie and Reg sit in their usual spots in the park. Alfie is Huddled in his sleeping bag sulking.

Silence.

Alfie: God it's cold.

> *[beat]*

> Seriously dude it's cold why is it so fucking cold?

Reg: Because the sun's gone in.

Alfie: You're funny... seriously how is it so cold? It's freaking summer and it's colder than when I first got here in March. How is that possible?

> *[Reg shrugs]*

> Aren't you cold?

> *[shrugs]*

> Great. Thanks...

Reg: Told you it didn't get any warmer.

Alfie: Yeah but I didn't think you were serious. It's summer. There's sun!

> *[Reg shrugs]*

> If I remember rightly you also said you get used to it. Well I'm not used to it. Look, my hands are like

purple, or blue or something I can't even see, it's dark. And how come it's dark already it's like six o-clock?

Reg: It's at least eight.

Alfie: How could you possibly know that?

Reg: Street lights came on a half hour ago.

Alfie: Oh... God I'm cold!

> *[Reg takes off the tatty, grey fingerless gloves he's been wearing and throws them to Alfie]*

Reg: There.

Alfie: Won't you get cold? *[Reg shrugs]* Wow dude, you're quiet today, even for you... *[puts the gloves on]* What's up?

Reg: Nothing.

Alfie: Ok.

> *[beat]*

Are you sure you're ok?

Reg: Yeah you?

Alfie: No I'm cold. And I'm hungry. I forgot to eat today. I woke up, took a piss, got some water and forgot to eat. I used to love breakfast. What happened? *[Reg shrugs]* Maybe that's my way of getting used to it. Getting used to being hungry.

Reg: Maybe.

Alfie: But now I've run out of food. Well I might have a biscuit or two but... my God I miss the days of inadvertent begging on a park bench...

Reg: Don't like...

Alfie: Don't like begging yeah I know. But it's got to be better than nothing. It's gotta be better than this.

Reg: You don't need to beg.

Alfie: Tell that to my empty stomach.

Reg: Here. *[pulls out a sandwich from underneath his rug and throws it to Alfie.]*

Alfie: Woah what the fuck? Can I really have this?

Reg: Yeah.

Alfie: You want to share?

Reg: Already ate.

Alfie: When?

Reg: Earlier.

Alfie: *[already tearing into the packet]* Jesus Reg smoked salmon and cream cheese, where did you get this?

Reg: Pret.

Alfie: Pret A Manger are you kidding? That place is like for rich people and bankers not even my Mum goes there! How did you get this?

Reg: Know a girl who works there, she gives me a few when she comes off shift, lets me pick before they go off to all the shelters.

Alfie: I've never seen you with a girl who works at Pret.

Reg: You've never seen me with anyone.

Alfie: Good point. Wait a minute, you won't beg but you're quite happy to go down to Pret and pick up their leftovers?

Reg: And?

Alfie: How is that not begging?

Reg: It's not begging.

Alfie: How?

Reg: Because she gives it to me, I don't ask.

Alfie: It's still charity.

Reg: It's not.

Alfie: It so is.

Reg: But it's not begging.

Alfie: So charity is different from begging?

Reg: Yeah. But it's not charity.

Alfie: Because...

Reg: Because it's not.

Alfie: And that's that then.

Reg: That's that.

Alfie: God you're so set in your ways.

Reg: What?

Alfie: You, you just are... so set. You have your things that you do, and you do them, and the things that you say, or don't say. And what you think or believe. You're just set. You've set yourself. You just... are.

Reg: So?

Alfie: So nothing, it's just what you are. I've noticed. I didn't mean to offend you...

Reg: You didn't offend me.

Alfie: Then why are you being so quiet?

Reg: I'm not.

Alfie: You are! Even more than usual.

Reg: I don't have anything to say.

Alfie: When do you ever? *[beat]* Don't you ever get bored? I mean I get bored and I've only been here a few months, and I've got you. I can't even imagine what it would be like on my own. And you were on your own weren't you? At least for a bit before I came. Did you ever have anyone else? Anyone like me to keep you company on the streets. Have you ever had a companion?

[Reg looks at Alfie who waits for him to respond. He doesn't]

Is that a yes?

Reg: There was an old guy once, Ron. He was around when I first got here. Then there was Ben, a couple of months ago.

Alfie: What happened to Ben? How come he's not still here?

Reg: Wasn't cut out for it.

Alfie: So he went home?

[Reg shrugs]

Do you think I'm cut out for this?

Reg: You tell me.

Alfie: When have I ever known the answer to any of my own questions? So what happened to Ron?

Reg: He died. A couple of years ago.

Alfie: Oh man, I'm sorry Reg. That must have really sucked.

Reg: Happens.

Alfie: So some people do this for life?

Reg: It's not a career Alfie.

Alfie: You know what I mean.

Reg: Yeah, some people are lifers.

Alfie: Are you a lifer?

Reg: Yeah.

Alfie: Don't you ever think about going home?

Reg: Don't have a home.

Alfie: But don't you ever think about going back? Finding the people you left behind? What if they're looking for you?

Reg: They're not.

Alfie: And what about starting fresh?

Reg: I just move on.

Alfie: But it's not the same is it? It's not the same as a home.

Reg: Like I said, it's not a career.

Alfie: Yeah. But is it a life?

Reg: What?

Alfie: I mean how many kids run around saying they wanna be a tramp when they're older? Think of all the shitty jobs kids want to do...bus driver, train driver, van driver, the guys at the zoo who clean out the animal poo. But even they know they don't want to be a tramp. So how do we get from there to here?

Reg: Some things just don't go to plan.

Alfie: But doesn't it make you wonder what if? What if you just hadn't have gone? What if you had stayed, or what if you went back now or found some help and built a new life? Don't you ever want to fall in love?

Reg: No.

Alfie: How can you say that though? How can you just let go of all that stuff? All those hopes and dreams you had when you were a kid? How can you possibly do that?

Reg: Just did.

Alfie: Just what?

Reg: Learnt to let go.

Alfie: So you really don't have any plans? You really are in this for life?

Reg: Guess so.

Alfie: And doesn't that make you sad? Sometimes, doesn't that make you sad?

Reg: No.

Alfie: How?

Reg: I don't care.

Alfie: What? How?

Reg: I just don't care.

Alfie: You do Reg. You must do. You don't have to care about what people think or how they look at you. You don't have to care about the fact you need to get handouts from strangers because you don't have enough money to walk into a shop and buy a sandwich. You don't have to have the biggest dreams. But when someone shouts tramp at you in the street or calls you worthless enough times, it gets to you. You wouldn't be human if it didn't. I've been here a few months and it gets to me, and I know you say you grow a thick skin but some things just can't be blocked out. And this shit can't be blocked out. And you know why? Because deep down we both know it's true. Deep down we both know they're right. Because they must be. Why on earth would they bother shouting that to a stranger if it wasn't true? Why is it that people feel like they can steal our belongings or kick us in our sleep if we aren't absolutely worthless? It's because they know they can go home Reg. They know they're a part of it all, and we're not. Some of them have shitty houses and shit jobs, some of them don't have jobs at all, but they know they're better than us because at least they have a bed. You were right Reg, we are the scum of the earth, and there's nothing we can do about it. It's not a name you earn by what you do or the person you aspire to be, it's a status you fall to. We're the ultimate fucking underclass, we're beyond the underclass we don't have a status at all because we're not even on the grid. No status granted if you don't have a fucking postal address. But I was on the grid once. And so were you. And we had our place and it was shit and we hated our lives because we weren't living it for ourselves but at least we were on the grid! At least we had a name and a national insurance number and a local GP and a bed and a pillow. At least we had a fucking pillow Reg. And now we don't have a fucking pillow, because some little shit stole mine, and God knows what happened to yours. God knows how long you've been sleeping on the ground! And it's shit. And we know it's shit. It's not the company, or the cold, or the bland repetition of day-in, day-out monotony and sitting around, it's not the food, or the fact we have to wash in a public toilet and dry ourselves under the hand dryers. It's not the weather or the harshness or the bitter disappointment of the dreams we once had...it's the fact that we don't exist. We don't fucking exist. We are nothing, absolutely nothing to the world except for some kind of disease.

[by now Alfie is beginning to sob]

We are nothing Reg. We don't exist. I don't exist. I don't exist Reg I don't exist. I used to exist and I used to hate it but at least I used to exist. And now... now I don't and, and... now I am nothing and, and I used to exist Reg, I need to exist! God Reg I need to exist!

[Alfie cries. Reg neither moves nor comments. He just sits there, present and unflinching until Alfie stops crying and begins to regain some control]

Reg... I don't think I'm cut out for this.

Scene 6.

The park, afternoon. Reg sits in his 'spot' looking out into the distance with a blank look on his face.

Alfie enters from stage right. He is wearing different clothes. He looks cleaner, better presented. He looks like a man who doesn't live on the streets. He carries with him a plastic bag of food.

He stops and looks at Reg who turns and faces him.

Alfie: Hi.

Reg: Hi.

Alfie: How've you been? Do you mind if I...

>*[Reg shrugs and makes a small gesture to Alfie to sit down]*

Thanks.

>*[Alfie takes off his jacket and lays it on the floor next to Reg, near where his 'spot' used to be. He sits.]*

So... it's been what, a few weeks now since, you know... maybe even... gosh has it really been a month? Strange it feels like longer. Or not, you know. Time kind of moves at a different pace around here, sometimes it's hard to readjust.

>*[beat]*

How have you been?

Reg: Fine. You?

Alfie: I've been, well I've been... fine.

Reg: You got new clothes.

Alfie: Yeah, pretty swish eh? My mum took me shopping for a new wardrobe said it was 'bonding time' but I think she's just trying to keep me busy, make sure I don't like, leave again. Or maybe she's just trying to remind me what I've been missing. She keeps mentioning all these things we have – they all do – and she's all "ooo I couldn't live without this and that" and then she'll look at me all pointedly as if she's waiting for me to agree. As if all it would take is a new shirt to keep me there. It's funny though, of all the things; getting my iPod back, nice new clothes, going out for meals, even getting to sleep on a fucking pillow again; of all the things I missed when I was out here – the first shower, that was the best. Just that feeling, of the water hitting my face, it was just so warm. The pressure on my body... it was like it washed everything away. And the towels were so soft. Everything just seemed so much softer, like I was clean. God listen to me going on about towels! I'm such a sell-out. I guess they got me. I guess I got bought.

Reg: It's not a crime to be bought.

Alfie: But it's not exactly courageous either. After all that time living here, to just go back and carry on like it never happened. They don't talk about it, none of them do. It's like the day after I came back they all decided to just forget it ever happened, to block it all out. But I don't want to forget. I don't think it's something that should be forgotten. I think it was too big for that. Not just because I was gone and I chose to go but because of what it meant. They just don't understand it. They don't get how good it can be... I guess it's not their world.

[pause]

Reg: You going back to Uni?

Alfie: Yeah. I know, it wasn't what I wanted, but I'm going back. I'm starting again and I'm going to study engineering. I'm going to join the Marines.

Reg: But you like English and books.

Alfie: Yeah I do. But engineering will look better for the Marines.

Reg: Why?

Alfie: Because it's more specialist – more suited for the job. And it's not a namby pamby subject for lawyers and queers.

Reg: It's not queer.

Alfie: No. But that's not what my Dad would say.

Reg: You still don't want to join the Marines.

Alfie: Question or statement?

Reg: Both.

Alfie: No I don't, you're right. But I need to do it for my family. I've already let them down enough; I need to do this for them.

Reg: Ok.

Alfie: Hey I've got something of yours. *[rummages in his pocket and pulls out Reg's gloves]* I don't know why I still have them, here.

Reg: You keep them.

Alfie: No really, take them. It'll be autumn soon, you'll need to keep warm. Besides, my Mum will probably take me shopping to buy some new ones anyway. Probably some high-fashion ones to remind me how amazing your hands can feel in a brand. *[hands Reg the gloves]* Oh and I brought these from home too. It's just a couple of things I found around the house and a chocolate bar I got from the Sainsbury's down the road. There's some toothpaste in there too, it's opened but still...

[Alfie hands the bag to Reg who looks in]

Reg: Thanks.

Alfie: It's the least I could do. It's hardly a salmon sandwich from Pret but it should fill a hole or two. There's some sausage rolls in there, and a couple of packs of crisps.

[Reg takes out the chocolate bar, opens it and hands Alfie two squares]

Thanks.

[They sit and eat in silence, each looking out at the park]

You know I still think about this place. And you. Everything that did or didn't happen in this spot. It stayed with me, it always will I'm sure of it. Sometimes I sit and wonder what it was that brought me here, to this exact spot, next to you. Why here, why now and why you? No matter how much stuff I have to do something always brings my mind back here. And sometimes I miss it. And I think you're very brave. I think you're very brave in everything you do and I admire that I really do admire that. I think it must be lonely being you, being that brave, but I think it's good. I think it would be a good thing to be you, and I think it's been a good thing in my life to have got to know you. I think you're one of the, the truest people I've ever met and you're just... strong. And I just, I wanted you to know that, how strong you are and you are so very strong and... God do I ever shut up?

Reg: No.

Alfie: Haha, no. You're right. That's another thing, you're always right.

Reg: Not all the time.

Alfie: Most of the time. Like I said, you just kind of... are.

[a silence falls again as the two men continue to look out over the park]

You know there's a point in the day where conversation sort of ends with you...

Reg: Yeah.

Alfie: Even I don't have anything more to say.

Reg: Yeah?

Alfie: I guess it kind of all just gets said, and anything else is just... futile.

[silence again, broken in a few seconds by the sound of Alfie's phone receiving a text. He jumps, pulls out his phone from his pocket and opens the text]

God I'm still not used to this whole having a phone thing again. I kind of forgot how much we all rely on them.

Reg: Is it new?

Alfie: No actually, this is the same one I had when I was here. I still never have any battery!

[reads the text]

It's my brother, he wants to meet me tonight.

Reg: You see him more now?

Alfie: Yeah.

Reg: That's nice.

Alfie: Yeah. He's definitely putting more effort in this time. I think he's realised how tough things were before, and he probably wants to keep an eye on me like everyone else. He was so excited when I told him I was joining the Marines. It's like I've become the little brother he always wanted me to be. Still... Well I'd better go. It's a decent journey to Portsmouth and the trains don't run that often. *[checks watch]* If I rush off I should make the next train.

[Alfie stands and picks up his coat off the floor]

You know what, here take this.

[he takes his watch off and holds it out to Reg who looks at it and frowns]

Seriously dude, take it. It was cheap I can get another one, and that way you won't have to go by the street lamps to tell the time. Please it's not charity it's a gift. Take it. To remind you of me.

[Reg takes the watch and Alfie smiles]

Reg: Thanks.

Alfie: It's the least I could do. You looked out for me. I'll always be grateful for that. And I want to come visit again, one day when I have the time, and if you're still here. I want to come visit again. I'm never going to forget...

[they look at each other for a moment, everything already said]

Right well, I'd better go. See you around Reg. Stay safe.

[Alfie turns and begins to walk away]

Reg: Alfie...

[Alfie stops and turns to Reg]

Good luck.

END